COULD THIS BE YOU?

How to Catch your Dream Creative Job

Ali Sparkes

Illustrated by **Selom Sunu**

OXFORD
UNIVERSITY PRESS

Letter from the Author

I usually write fiction, and have a great time making things up for living – but sometimes I want to write about stuff that is totally real.

I meet lots of children and young people in schools and I can tell sometimes that they think having this cool job of being an author is somehow SO FAR REMOVED from them.

But it's not. Not so very long ago, I would never have dreamed I would write books for a living. Well, maybe I would have *dreamed* it – I was a very dreamy child – but I certainly wouldn't have imagined it could really happen to me. I wasn't super clever. I didn't get loads of As in class … or in any exam I ever took. I didn't go to university. But I did have a great passion for reading and, eventually, for writing.

The thing is, if someone had told me what being an author was *really* like, and given me a list of things to do that could help me become one, I *might* have got my first book published a lot sooner. So that's why I put my next epic adventure story on hold, just long enough to write this book. Just in case *you* might need that information – and that useful checklist – about *your* dream job. I hope it helps.

Now, back to the fiction. I think I left an imaginary ten-year-old dangling off a cliff somewhere …

Ali Sparkes

Contents

Could This Be You? 4
Could You Be an Author? 5
Could You Be an Illustrator? 9
Could You Be a Singer? 14
Could You Be a Dancer? 19
Could You Be a Fashion Designer? 24
Could You Be an Actor? 29
Could You Be a TV or Film Director? 34
Could You Be a Radio Presenter? 39
Fail, Fail and Fail Again! 44
Glossary 46
Index 48

The glossary

Some words in this book are in **bold**. When you read a **bold** word, think about what it means. If you don't know, you can look it up in the glossary at the end of the book.

Could This Be You?

Hey, you. *You*, holding this book right now. Have you been asked THAT question yet? You know ... 'What do you want to be when you grow up?'

OK, I know, I know. You get asked it ALL THE TIME. I used to say, 'A bit taller than I am now.'

Maybe you already know. Maybe you're still making up your mind. Maybe you haven't got a clue yet, and just wish this paragraph didn't have so many maybes.

If you're an imaginative, creative or artistic type, thinking about how you might get your dream job could be half the battle. But being creative doesn't mean you can't also be driven, practical and focused – if you want that job *enough*.

In this book, you can read about some of the creative jobs many people dream of doing, and get the inside story from people who actually do them. You'll also get some tips on what to do NOW to make getting your dream job more feasible in the future. Read on to find out ...

Could You Be an Author?

You love reading. Of *course* you do: you're reading THIS! Maybe you enjoy writing stories, too. Could you do this for a job? I'm doing it right now, writing *this*, so you might as well ask me, Ali Sparkes. I mostly write fiction. You might have read my *Shapeshifter* series, *Frozen in Time*, *Car-Jacked* or about fifty other books I've had published.

Q What's it really like, being an author?

It's a strange world, because I daydream for a living. At school, I was often told off for staring dreamily out of the window. If only I had *known* that one day it would be my job! I could have said, 'Look, I'm preparing myself for a successful career as an author!' (I don't think that would have got me out of Physics, though …)

To write a book, I come up with ideas and I tease them out into characters and plots and big adventures. I also have to do some real-world research. For a book called *Dark Summer*, I researched the caves at Wookey Hole in Somerset, and got to see the hidden areas where the public don't usually go. I loved it! For *Frozen in Time*, I had to investigate life in the 1950s, which was fascinating. I also do presentations about my books and writing at schools and **literary festivals**, so I'm a bit of a performer too.

> I love those writing days when it's going so well that I forget who I am: I'm just IN the story, BEING the characters.

Q What's a working day like for you?

On a writing day, I usually start by taking my dog (a big woolly labradoodle called Willow) out for a walk. A lot of my story-making happens in my head, when I'm nowhere near a keyboard.

Then, after breakfast, I'll go up to my writing place at the end of the garden. I call it the 'POD' – which stands for 'Place Of Dreams'. It's small, cosy and peaceful. I'm in it as I write *this*! I seldom write for more than a couple of hours in a day. Close to a deadline, though, I can write all day – which is EXHAUSTING!

I might just as easily be running workshops at a school or on stage at a big literary festival, though. That can be quite nerve-wracking, but I really love it.

Q How did you get into it?

I always loved writing stories when I was at school, but my main ambition was to be an actor and singer in musicals. Sadly, that didn't work out. (Why? Why? WHY?) Much less sadly, though, I ended up working as a local newspaper reporter – which was just brilliant! I learned how to interview people and get them to tell me stuff, and then to turn my notes into a news story or **feature**. This was such a good grounding. Without it, you wouldn't be reading this book right now, because I would never have written it!

Then I moved into radio, working with the **BBC** as a **broadcast journalist**, which was also fantastic – hard work and scary, but exciting. You really learn to think on your feet in live radio because, if it goes wrong, thousands of people are listening. There's nowhere to hide! (You can read more about this from Andy Bennett on pages 39–43.)

Along the way, I started up a magazine for the radio station and also wrote and recorded little bits of comedy for BBC Radio 4. I sent some story ideas off to **publishers** and **agents** and – after about three or four years of rejections – finally got an agent and a book deal with Oxford University Press, for the *Shapeshifter* series.

Q What do you love most about it?

I love knowing that a wild idea I'm having could end up as a book read by many thousands of children – and adults – around the world. I love those writing days when it's going so well that I forget who I am: I'm just IN the story, BEING the characters.

And I love sharing what I do with audiences in schools and book festivals and – most of all – making them laugh.

Q What don't you like about it?

It's quite unstable: you don't get paid a regular salary. Sometimes the money from your **royalties** is really good – and other times it's really bad, and that can be worrying.

And your book can still get rejected at any time. You might think you've written the best story in the world, but nobody seems to agree with you. That can be tough.

Q What can I do NOW to get into a writing career?

Read and read and read. Experiment with lots of different authors and different styles. As you read, you'll be absorbing what works in a story. Then start writing. Enter writing competitions. Polish and edit your work. Investigate any writing workshops you can join after school or during holidays. Collaborate with friends and make comics and magazines and **scripts**. Write for fun!

Don't worry about writing a full-length book just yet. It takes time to build your skills and your 'voice' as a writer. You don't need to hurry. If you're a writer, you WILL write. You won't be able to help it.

And don't be downhearted if your story gets rejected by a publisher. Everyone gets rejected, usually many times, before they get some success!

WRITING CHECKLIST:
- Read a lot of books, in different genres.
- Start writing in any way you like.
- Write with friends.
- Enter writing competitions.
- Don't hurry and don't worry — becoming a good writer takes time, and rejections!

Could You Be an Illustrator?

Do you doodle? Is drawing your thing? If so, you might be thinking about a job as a book illustrator. Selom Sunu has illustrated *this very book* – so he was the obvious choice to ask about his job.

I applied for a Master's degree in animation ... and didn't get on it! But they said I should try again next year and, while I waited, I should draw every day: go to the zoo and draw animals.

Q What's it really like, being an illustrator?

People might think it's easy and a bit of fun. It is really interesting and varied but it can be demanding. Sometimes all you want is to sit down and focus, but you've got things on your mind so it's not easy. You don't always have an idea straight away. Sometimes you have to do a lot of digging and extra reading and search for inspiration.

Q What's a working day like for you?

For a book, I might be reading the manuscript or maybe researching what the characters might look like, finding images online for inspiration.

I like to start with my sketch book, in pencil. I start off with quite a few variations of the character to see which one works best. Then, once I'm happy with it, I take it into my digital drawing software, make corrections and add colour. A normal day is spent mostly doing that, at home with a computer and a drawing tablet.

Q How did you get into it?

When I was about seven, I remember drawing Biff, Chip and Kipper from the Oxford Reading Tree books. My teacher was really impressed and encouraged me to keep going.

We had to draw portraits in art and I drew my friends, Billy and Sam – and my teachers really loved them. These were just pencil **caricatures** but they ended up being up on the wall in school. The deputy headteacher congratulated me!

When I was eleven, though, we left London and went to Ghana – and there wasn't any formal art education in my school there. I had a couple of lessons with an artist outside of school, but it was fine art and painting, and I always enjoyed drawing cartoons. I didn't really connect – and it was a time when I was more interested in playing football!

I came back to England at 14 and did GCSE Art, but I had some catching up to do. I got a bit discouraged; I didn't get great results. I did Art at A-level but I got **disillusioned** so I did a Business Studies and Marketing degree at university.

Then I got a job with a charity. It was quite boring, so I would just doodle on a sticky note from time to time! Colleagues would say, 'That's really good', and I started thinking about taking up drawing again. Then, while I was back in Ghana on holiday, I had an idea for a book – but I knew nothing about illustration, so I found a short course on illustration at a college called Central St Martin's in London.

After that, I applied for a Master's degree in animation ... and didn't get on it! But they said I should try again next year and, while I waited, I should draw every day: go to the zoo and draw animals. I'd also draw people on the train. It was all very hard work – but, after a year, I went back ... and I was in!

I had to work a morning shift from six to ten at a cafe every day and then go into college. I'd draw my colleagues at the cafe from time to time.

My first commission was a book, and I was asked to do the artwork for its social media and animation, too. I was so naive that I took very little money for a lot of work, which affected my ability to take on other work. You live and learn!

Then I got an **internship** at an animation studio. It didn't involve drawing – it was the more computerized end of animation. I got a full-time job there ... but then got sacked because I was too slow at it.

I went back to working for charities, but was asked to do the cover of a book called *Ghost*, by Jason Reynolds. They hired me to do the covers for the whole series. I got myself an agent, but it still took a while to get more work. I did a lot of sample drawing and it was, 'No, no, no ... '

But lots of good things have happened since then!

Q What do you love most about it?

I'm especially keen on characters: finding new ways of designing people. I love people-watching anyway. I love creating different faces.

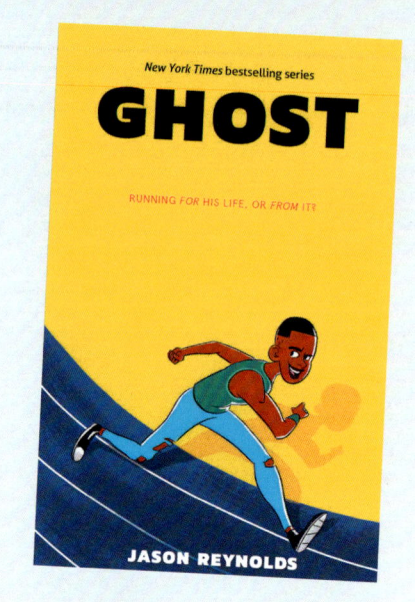

Q What don't you like about it?

The revisions: when you have to redo your drawings for a client. I once spent about eighty hours on this one **spread** – back and forth, back and forth, back and forth. I thought I was finished but then they came back *again* and I just thought, 'NOOOOOO!'

It can also be quite lonely, working by myself. I'm the one who has to motivate myself. It's not like there's a team behind me that I can bounce ideas off.

Q What can I do NOW to get into illustrating?

Start with copying other illustrators and any work you like. It will help you develop your own style.

Draw lots and try to draw things from real life. Start with plants and objects rather than living people ... unless you have someone who is willing to sit still for you!

ILLUSTRATING CHECKLIST:

- Draw A LOT!
- Copy the drawings you like.
- Draw animals: visit the zoo or the local park with your sketch pad, or look at animals online.
- Draw your friends (if they'll keep still).
- Look out for art competitions to enter.
- Check out courses at college that would suit you best. (Don't get graphic design or animation confused with fine art, as they vary a lot!)

Could You Be a Singer?

We hear singers constantly – on TV, radio, adverts, films and stage. Do you sing? Is this something you could do for a living?

You may have heard Hayley Sanderson. Hayley is best known for being one of the singers with Dave Arch's orchestra on the BBC's *Strictly Come Dancing*: a massively popular TV show in the UK.

> I love that one day I can be on Strictly, and the next day I'm on stage under my own name, singing songs that I can choose.

Q What's it really like, being a singer?

Most people think it's glamorous, which it can be – but it's also hard work, long hours, intense and pressured! There are a lot of fun elements as well, but I think people only see the glamour. In reality, it's just lots of rehearsing.

I love the variety, especially with *Strictly*, because so many different styles of music are involved: a Cuban song or a jazz piece one minute, and the next minute you could be singing a song by Shirley Bassey or Kylie Minogue.

The show is all about the dancers, so you have to be exact on phrasing and timing to give them the rhythm they need. I read sheet music, but we don't often use it for *Strictly*. They want you to sound natural and, when you're reading, it can *sound* like you're reading. We do get the sheet music, though, if it's a complicated jazz harmony thing or something quite demanding in musical theatre week.

Q What's a working day like for you?

Strictly takes up about six months of my year, including a live tour, but while it's on TV I'll also be out doing **session work** for other people during the week. My working day with *Strictly* starts when all the singers rehearse together on a Friday evening.

The songs are sent to us beforehand and we learn them. I'll work out *all* the harmonies because I never know what part I may need to change when I get to the rehearsal. Then we all arrive on a Friday evening. The singers get together first, and we rehearse for an hour to make sure we've got our parts right. The first time we rehearse as a band is on the Friday night for the show on Saturday. On the Saturday morning, the dancers rehearse with us – then we go live on Saturday night.

After the live show, we have to wait for the audience votes to come in before we pre-record the Sunday results show – so we record it really late, and everyone's a bit tired.

Q How did you get into it?

I started doing musical theatre when I was about seven. My uncle was in a soul band so I'd go and watch him, and he got me into listening to old soul and jazz records. Then, when I was twelve, I won some money in a singing competition and bought a **PA system**, and started singing in local venues.

I did lots of performances at our local theatre, and then I joined a girl band called Ruby Fusion (it was a terrible name!) and moved to London. That's where I met lots of other musicians because we worked with them to do the live gigs.

I used to **arrange** all the backing vocals for the band, as well as write the songs. We worked with some amazing people – and when Ruby Fusion finally failed to get anywhere, I got back in touch with those people and said, 'I want to work in the industry – what can I do?'

Q What do you love most about it?

I love that one day I can be on *Strictly*, and the next day I'm on stage under my own name, singing songs that I can choose. The next day I might be doing backing vocals for Jennifer Hudson, and the next day after that I might be in the studio, doing a jingle for a breakfast cereal advert. It's so extreme!

And I've worked with some amazing people like Ellie Goulding, CeeLo Green, Nile Rodgers and John Legend.

Q What don't you like about it?

The awkward hours and the time away: I've not been with my friends or family on my birthday for 20 years. Sometimes you'll drive for several hours and then set up and rehearse and get ready – and the gig's only an hour, and then you go home.

Q What can I do NOW to become a singer?

Listen to as much music as possible, and don't just pay attention to the vocalist. Listen to the backing vocals, the way the **instrumentation** is put together, the bass, the guitar, the **root notes** – that's so important.

Then sing! Get into a choir or start a band with some friends. Study your favourite singers in online videos but don't focus on just *one* singer. When I was younger, I was really into singers like Mariah Carey. My uncle said I should listen to who *they* listened to. He gave me my first Ella Fitzgerald CDs. I learned so much from them!

Learn to read music, too: you'll need that if you work as a session singer in studios. And look after your voice. Drink lots of water and warm up before you perform. Warming up in the car on the way to a gig works well!

SINGING CHECKLIST:

- Start performing in school choirs and shows.
- Listen to all kinds of singers.
- Learn to read music.
- Get your own band together.
- Look out for auditions and go for them (and don't be upset if you don't get them — everyone fails along the way).

Could You Be a Dancer?

Do you dance around the kitchen? Practise your moves by the mirror? Then maybe this is your thing ...

Ballet is one of the most athletic forms of dance – and mesmerizing to watch on stage! Steven McRae is a principal dancer with The Royal Ballet and has danced lead roles in ballet all over the world. He's also a brilliant **tap-dancer** and performs his own **choreography**. You can see him as Skimbleshanks in the 2019 film *Cats*.

> I was a tiger unleashed for that hour. It was the most sensational feeling.

Q What's it really like, being a dancer?

Many people think you turn up at the theatre maybe an hour before the show, pop on your costume, do your thing and then go home – but we very often work twelve-hour days.

Dance has literally taken me all around the world. It's helped me to meet so many incredible people. I grew up in a small suburb of Sydney, Australia, and I wasn't from an artistic family whatsoever. To be suddenly on the other side of the world and performing at Buckingham Palace in front of the Queen, or having dinner with Prince Charles at a function raising money for The Royal Ballet – things like this would just not happen where I grew up. That was unheard of.

Q **What's a working day like for you?**

We start at half past nine or half past ten in the morning, and if there's an evening performance we'll work until half past five. Then there's a two-hour break to eat and put on make-up. The performance usually starts at half past seven and finishes at half past ten.

The day-to-day process of creating a ballet is much more brutal than the public would probably ever imagine, because obviously they see the finished product, which is very polished and slick. The job, particularly for ballet dancers, is to make it all look effortless ... but it is extremely demanding.

It's a highly critical profession, and it requires a certain **mindset** to be able to cope with that. You're looking in the mirror as you dance, every single day, and all you see are the faults – and obviously coaches are there to help you get better so they tell you what was *wrong* most of the time, not necessarily what was good!

But it's an extraordinary world to be a part of. You get to do something you're passionate about, and you get paid to do it.

Q How did you get into it?

My dad worked in motorsports, so I was brought up at the racetrack. Dance wasn't something that anybody predicted I would get into. After seeing my sister dance one day, though, I said I'd like to have a go. I was incredibly shy: I wouldn't speak to anybody, let alone get up and dance in front of anybody, so I think Mum and Dad thought it would only last a week.

But I was absolutely hooked. I can remember what that first lesson felt like. I was seven years old. It was jazz dance – loud music, kicks, jumps, spinning around. I was a tiger unleashed for that hour. It was the most sensational feeling.

After about six months, the teacher said, 'Why don't you try a bit of ballet and a bit of tap?' By the age of nine, I was dancing six days a week – every day after school, all day Saturday. I just loved it.

At 17, I went to the Prix de Lausanne: an international competition for young dancers in Switzerland. First place would take the winner to The Royal Ballet School. I won the competition – and the next day I flew straight to London, because we couldn't afford to first go back to Australia and then fly to Europe again when school started.

Q What do you love most about it?

Dance is a universal language: we use our bodies as our voices. I can perform anywhere in the world and make the audience walk out of that theatre feeling different – and I've not said a single word. There are no barriers with dance.

Q What don't you like about it?

You have to give everything. I had to move away from my family to the other side of the world to pursue my career. Your health, quite often, can be put aside just to get through a show, even though you know you should stop. You don't want to let people down, and you don't want to miss out.

I once snapped my **Achilles tendon** on stage in front of the whole Royal Opera House audience. It was just me on stage, performing – and it went BANG. I managed to stay upright, but I couldn't stand on the leg; my foot wasn't responding. The orchestra kept going and then eventually they brought the curtain in and the orchestra stopped. The audience sat in silence, listening to me screaming behind the curtain because I was in agony. It felt like somebody had stuck a knife into my leg.

But injuries are part of the profession, and we have a huge medical team at the Opera House. Dancing twelve hours a day, six days a week, your body is going to experience wear and tear.

Q What do I need to do NOW to get into dancing?

Even if you're thinking ballet is what you want to do, what you *have* to do, what you're *going* to do, you still need to explore other styles. Go on the Internet and find a video of somebody tap-dancing and just learn thirty seconds of that. Break it down, and do five seconds each day. It'll set you up really well for a career in dance.

Choreographers need dancers to be like chameleons: they want you to do this style or that style. Explore many different styles and be that chameleon!

DANCING CHECKLIST:

- Start NOW. It's never too soon. This applies to *any* kind of dance, not just ballet or tap.
- Be ready to put the hours in — it takes time to get good.
- Try lots of different styles, not just one.
- Look after your health so you can keep dancing.
- Be ready to learn from criticism and don't take it personally.

Could You Be a Fashion Designer?

Do you LOVE clothes? Do you scour magazines for pictures of the stars wearing all the latest designs? Maybe you love drawing, too – you might have sketched a few of your own designs, or even had a go at making some clothes.

But could you design clothes for a job? That's what Charlotte Allen – the creator of **womenswear** brand Klements – had to find out for herself.

Q What's it really like, being a fashion designer?

People may think fashion designers just sit around drawing beautiful shapes and dresses and being creative and magical, while interesting celebrities are coming and going.

In reality, there's lots of **admin**, maths, working out prices and costs, emails, packing orders, dealing with **logistics** and post and **invoices** ... But then you have the great days when you do the photo shoot or a celebrity wears something you designed, and you get to put it on social media, and then you sell lots!

I sent out samples to different stores – and **Harrods** called me. To get your clothes into Harrods on your first go is pretty exciting!

Q What's a working day like for you?

Well, on a boring day I'll be cracking on with emails, sorting out orders or returns, working out how much fabric to buy and adding up the costs on the calculator. I might have to race off to one of the factories because there's a problem with a pattern that they're printing onto fabric for me. That kind of problem can cost me money, because it holds up production of the clothes.

A good day is when I've blocked time out in the studio and I'm just sitting down painting flowers (I paint my designs by hand first). Or I might be researching ideas in books, or maybe going to an exhibition and getting inspired – then I'll come back and put all that inspiration into the work.

A photo shoot, for me, is the ultimate achievement. I get to see all that work coming together: all the prints I've designed now made into garments, all lined up on the clothes rail. I can decide what the model's going to wear – I can lay things out, and style them in certain ways. You get these amazing images that you know you're going to be using to advertise your **collection**, and you come back and feel completely full of satisfaction.

Q How did you get into it?

When I was nine or ten, I was sketching dresses and drawing shapes and coming up with names for my own fashion **label**.

As a teenager, I couldn't afford clothes in the shops so I bought the fabric and made my own things. I once made a skirt with a big safety pin in – and, when I came to wear it, it just fell down! The next time I made a skirt, I realized what I needed to do to make sure it stayed up!

We had a sewing machine at home. We'd been taught how to use them at school, and I just practised. I went to art college to do fine art and be a portrait painter – but then decided to do a **textiles** and fashion degree.

My first job was as a wallpaper designer, and after that I worked for a company in Leicester, designing for various clothing brands. Then I got a scholarship for a Master's degree. I made a collection as a student that I was really proud of, and a designer spotted it and offered me a job – and I went to work for their brand as a print designer.

I knew I wanted to launch my own label, but I needed money for that. So after a few years, I started doing some freelance print design for some high-street fashion brands and I set up Klements on the side, just selling scarves, to test the market. My scarves sold really well, so I started doing printed womenswear.

Later, I got a sales agent out in the US and my designs sold to about fifty shops all across America. I would go out there and do road trips, starting in Seattle and driving down to Los Angeles, stopping off at stores along the way. That's a lovely part of the job, mixing travel with work.

I sent out samples to different stores – and *Harrods* called me. To get your clothes into Harrods on your first go is pretty exciting!

Q What do you love most about it?

Photo shoots and drawing! I also like to pack my orders myself, which is quite unusual at my level – but, when orders come in, I look at a map online and see they've come from the middle of Hawaii or Arizona and I'll pack the order up with a little note to the customer. Some customers have become my friends, dotted around the world, who write to me regularly.

And sometimes celebrities wear my designs!

Q What don't you like about it?

It's very competitive. You're doing your own thing and then you look at another designer's work and you think, 'Oh, why didn't I do that?' You work very hard – evenings and weekends.

Then there's **cash flow**. When you've designed a collection, you've got to have it manufactured; it's going to cost a certain amount of money to get that done. That's quite scary. Then your collection *has* to sell. It has to make money for your label to survive.

Q What can I do NOW to get into designing?

Start experimenting with fashion now: you have to learn a lot. Learn to sew and work on your art – and study! People assume fashion is all quite frivolous, but actually designers are very clever. A really good designer has to understand art, art history and film, to pick up cultural references from many different places and times.

DESIGNING CHECKLIST:

- Work on your art.
- Learn to sew.
- Investigate fashion design in books, online and in films.
- Look into art history.
- Be ready to work hard!

Could You Be an Actor?

You've seen actors in all your favourite TV shows and movies. Are you thinking, 'I could do that'?

Meet Hiba Chader. She thought that, too – and it turns out she was right! Her biggest role so far has been in a children's TV series called *Secret Life of Boys*, playing the role of Hiba (yes – same name!) but she's also been in a film with Rowan Atkinson, and in adverts and online games.

> Watching my films or episodes later and knowing that all that hard work paid off – that's a lot of fun.

Q What's it really like, being an actor?

Most people think you're the centre of attention the whole day, and it's the best thing in the world. It IS the best thing – but most acting is not like Hollywood! It requires a lot of hard work and dedication.

You have to learn your lines and you slowly start falling into the character once you've played them for a bit. You read through the script a few times and get a feel for the scene – but once you're on **set** you just *become* the character, because everything's set up, you're in the costume and it all starts flowing.

It's not just about saying the lines. There's the timing: where you're looking, *when* you're looking, your body language, where you're standing – and you have to remember all this because people can't keep telling you, 'Take a step back, go forward, go to the side …' every five seconds. You need to figure it out for yourself.

Q What's a working day like for you?

Usually I have to be up at 6 am, and it's like this:

1. Get up, shower, wash my hair and have breakfast.
2. Take my clothes and everything else I need, and travel to the set.
3. Arrive at the set and wait in the **green room**. Often I'll be doing school work with a tutor while I wait – it's a legal requirement here when you're still school age.
4. Go to get my hair and make-up done.
5. Put my costume on.
6. Sit around for about twenty minutes while they check my hair, make up and costume. The most annoying part is that there's always such a rush to get ready – and then they leave me waiting for about two hours!
7. Go up on set, where they'll probably be adjusting the cameras.
8. Have more checks for hair and make-up, checks for the costume, checks for the camera, checks for the microphone, checks for the set ... and then, at last, this is the acting bit and I *finally* start filming.
9. Get off set, take my make-up and costume off, and then travel home ... and do it all again tomorrow.

Q How did you get into it?

By chance, when I was 10. We moved to a house near a theatre and heard about an **open call** audition for a role in a play called *The Grapes of Wrath*.

I'd never thought about acting, but my mum treated it as a free drama workshop so my little sister Rumaysa and I went along. I was so intimidated, because all the other kids at the audition did drama and they'd done a lot of shows – and I hadn't – but a week later I got a call saying I'd got the job!

Then I got spotted by a talent agent who came to see the play. Once I was with the agency, I started getting jobs.

My first job was acting in videos created to teach young children English. We had to re-record videos again and again to get the speed just right. It was so difficult. It was three days of filming, eight hours with one hour break every day.

Then I got an audition for an advert for a well-known brand of doll. In the scene, I had to ride a horse. That was the decider: it was between me and another girl, but she couldn't ride and I could.

Q **What do you love most about it?**

Getting to meet and work with such talented and incredible people (both cast and crew). I've met some really great friends on set! Also, watching my films or episodes later and knowing that all that hard work paid off – that's a lot of fun. Finally – I funded my own horse from my pay! She's an ex-professional **showjumper** so we do a lot of jumping.

Q **What don't you like about it?**

Getting things wrong really stresses me out. Once I was doing a taekwondo move and I couldn't land a particular kick.

The director said, 'Hiba, you have to get off set – you're getting too stressed!' I sat down for five minutes, got a drink of water, came back and landed it – and we got the shot.

Also, acting is not reliable at all. You may get loads of jobs for six months, and the next year you get nothing.

Q What can I do NOW to get into acting?

If your school does shows, try those – or a youth theatre, if there's one near you. Skills like horse riding and martial arts can really help you to get work in TV and film. Learning martial arts is also really good for your confidence. To get that TV work, though, you'll need an agent.

Learn to be **resilient** with auditions, too. Once, I *really* wanted a job but they chose another girl and I was so devastated. From that day, I decided never to make a big deal out of it again – because otherwise you'll just get hurt every single time.

If you get a job, you get it; if you don't, you don't. They may be looking for someone with curly hair, and that's what sets you apart – someone suits the look the director wanted for that role.

ACTING CHECKLIST:
- Start acting in school shows and local youth theatres, if there are any where you live.
- Work on martial arts and other skills, like singing, dancing and (if you can) horse riding.
- Be prepared for rejection at auditions, and don't take it personally.
- Try agencies for TV work.
- Learn to be patient: there are long waits on TV sets!

Could You Be a TV or Film Director?

You love great films! You love good TV! And *somebody* has to make that stuff. Somebody is directing from behind the camera and bringing stories to life for the screen. Could that be you?

Rebecca Rycroft thought maybe it could be her – and she was right. You may have seen some of the shows Rebecca has directed, like children's drama *Malory Towers* (based on the Enid Blyton books). Rebecca is now working on dramas, sitcoms and thrillers set all over the UK.

> When you're making a film, shorter is better – *always*. A film just needs thirty seconds to make it stand out and get attention, and from there things can happen.

Q What's it really like, being a director?

Most people think it's really glamorous, with amazing locations, famous actors and that I'm the only person making the decisions and telling everyone what to do! Sometimes it's like that, but it's actually about collaborating with amazing departments like design, costume and lighting – with people at the tops of their games, helping you make a brilliant project.

Q What's a working day like for you?

It's long!

5 am: I get up around now, depending on where we're filming.

7 am: I get to the set to discuss things with the First Assistant Director and Director of Photography (my key people), who plan the shoot with me.

8 am: Filming! We have to film around five to ten pages of scenes a day. It doesn't seem like a lot, but filming takes a long time! There's meant to be an hour for lunch, but I usually only find ten minutes to eat.

7 pm: I discuss the next day with the design team, check costume and make-up ideas, finalize what we need, and then talk to my editor about how scenes are working and what my original ideas were.

8 pm: I get home and watch the assemblies (sequences of scenes put together) from which I will choose a director's 'cut'. I also finalize filming plans for the next day.

12 am: Go to bed!

Then I do it all again for six or seven weeks!

Q How did you get into it?

I was the class fool, always wanting to make people laugh. I made a few films at art college, and then started working in the TV industry at 18. I worked mainly in comedy and with the support of some great **producers** and comedians, I worked my way up from **runner** to director. I had no qualifications – just an enthusiasm to work in TV or film and a passion for the shows I was working on.

There aren't many women directing TV or films, but in my twenties I worked with some amazing women who were high up in comedy on a brilliant show. Seeing women in these roles, making such an amazing show, influenced me to think that women could call the shots!

Q What do you love most about it?

Going to work and laughing every day, for a living! Reading brilliant, cleverly-written scripts and bringing those words off the page to life! Working with actors – helping them perform at their best, and making time to play and be creative to find the best way to make a scene.

And I love working with other women in film and TV (it can be quite male-dominated), and inspiring the next generation. I always encourage girls who are interested in filmmaking to visit the set. It's a great way for people to learn and see what I do.

Ella Bright, who plays Darrell in *Malory Towers*, has started making films herself and she's won a competition! She says seeing me working as a director inspired her.

I also enjoy being creative. It would be so easy to use the same formula, so I'm always pushing myself to try different things.

Q What don't you like about it?

The early mornings and the long hours!

Q What can I do NOW to get into directing?

If you have a phone, tablet or camera, start making videos. If you don't have your own, see if you can borrow one from school or from your family or friends – and just try. The more you try stuff, the more you'll learn.

You can also just take pictures and put them in a sequence. If you think about making a film, it's just putting one picture after the other. You can even draw your film with **storyboards** which is another way of doing it, and helps you plan!

When you're making a film, shorter is better – *always*. A film just needs thirty seconds to make it stand out and get attention, and from there things can happen. You *can* go to film school, of course, although I never did.

There are schemes for young filmmakers and some schools are now running film competitions which is really good, because it's a medium, it's art.

To get work in a **production company** is a tricky thing, but they do offer work experience, usually for two weeks at a time. Contact people you admire – via social media once you're old enough – and see if you can share your filmmaking that way.

DIRECTING CHECKLIST:

- Watch lots of different types of film and TV. See what inspires you most.
- Make short films with your friends using a phone or tablet.
- Create storyboards with drawings or photos.
- Look out for competitions to enter.
- Ask at your school, nearest cinema or arts centre about opportunities for young filmmakers. If there isn't a club, maybe you could set one up!
- Search online for national young filmmaker competitions.

Could You Be a Radio Presenter?

From discussing world events to introducing music tracks, radio presenting sounds like a cool job. But is it? Andy Bennett presents on BBC Radio Somerset in England. Here's what he thinks ...

When I was a kid, living on our family farm, I used to make my own radio shows out in the barn.

Q What's it really like, being a radio presenter?

It's wonderful – but when you're on air and that **mic** is live, you've got to sound like everything is under control and you're having a great day.

Off air, when the mic fader's down, it can be a nightmare, with a producer in your ear saying, 'That guest isn't here ... We can't go to that feature yet ... We haven't got that next section ready ... '

You've got to make it sound like it's a wonderful flowing river, when the whole time it can be very choppy!

Q What's a working day like for you?

Something like this:

10 am: I show up, log in and check emails. Is there any breaking news? Are there any interesting guests planned for the show?

10.15 am: A news editor will come to speak to me and my producer and say, 'Right, here's what the morning show has done; here's what the other shows have done; here's a thing you could do this afternoon.' That could be following on from an earlier item or a news thread that's running throughout the day.

10.30 am: We make calls and book guests. If you want someone to talk about recent flooding at half past four, you have to find them and book them in. Sometimes you've got interviews already lined up for the day, or you've recorded interviews beforehand and can play them on the radio, but you do have to respond to that day's news and find your lead items on the day. We write a loose script and questions for our guests, and get the audio together.

2 pm: I'm on air, which means we're live on the radio now! You could hear me if you were listening to the radio station.

Q How did you get into it?

When I was a kid, living on our family farm, I used to make my own radio shows out in the barn.

I'd plug in a microphone to an old radio and switch between radio and mic, fading out the radio before the DJ spoke so I could do the talking! I even cut my mother's bathroom sponge up to make a **microphone shield**.

It never came into my head that I would do it for a job. I never went to university and my career path went nowhere near radio presenting. I'm a trained agricultural **welder**. But, wherever I went to do my welding jobs, I'd always have the radio on. If I was using loud machinery but there was something good on the radio, I would wait until I'd heard that bit and then I'd go back to work.

I was working on building things for the Somerset Carnivals and for Glastonbury Festival (which are really big events in Somerset) – and, because someone at BBC Radio Somerset knew me, they'd ring me up to talk about it on air.

I ended up being a contributor on their radio show, maybe once a month. Then, when the BBC ran an apprenticeship scheme, everyone said I should go for it. It was only for six months and I'd have to take a massive pay cut, but I knew if I didn't take the chance I would spend the rest of my life wondering. So, I went for it … *And I never got the job.*

A few weeks later, though, I decided to email them again – and it turned out the guy who got the apprenticeship went on holiday to America and never came back. So I started to work at the BBC and I never left.

A permanent radio presenter job came up, and I got it.

Q **What do you love most about it?**

I've never had a day when it's felt like work. I get to talk to interesting people, from a celebrity to a local parish councillor. Every year, there's a 'Live in Somerset' event in Taunton, and I get to hang out backstage and go on stage and introduce amazing bands and performers. And I'm just a welder – having a chat with a superstar, in front of 11 000 people! I love that.

Q **What don't you like about it?**

The paperwork. A form has to be filled in for every song you play. If you go and do an interview, everything has to be risk assessed: 'Will you be struck by lightning while interviewing that lady on the farm?' Sometimes you feel you need a **hazmat suit** and a lawyer present!

And if you say something wrong, headbutt the microphone, play the wrong jingle, press the wrong button or the guest isn't there, you do get annoyed at yourself.

Q What do I need to do NOW to get into radio presenting?

Don't assume something is stopping you. If you want to be in radio, you need to listen to the radio and practise. Learn something about those songs: what would a DJ say for those thirty seconds between the tracks?

Practise talking to yourself! I used to be in a hay barn, on my own, talking to myself about songs I'd just heard on the radio. The more comfortable you can be talking, and the more radio you listen to, the better.

RADIO PRESENTING CHECKLIST:

- Listen to lots of radio and practise talking between tracks.
- Interview your friends as if you were live on air.
- Record your interviews, if you can, and learn to edit them.
- When you're older, ask about opportunities at a radio station near you.

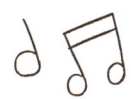

Fail, Fail and Fail Again!

One common thread you might have noticed all the way through this book is FAILURE. Failure is important. It's hard to see it as a good thing when you've just failed to get on a course, crashed out of an audition or had your PERFECT book rejected (*again*) but trust me, if you never fail, you'll never be as good as you can be.

Before I got my first book deal, I had FOUR YEARS of rejections. *(Whimper.)* The rejections weren't all horrible, and some of them were *very nearly not* rejections. Sometimes, like Hiba in her acting auditions, my book just wasn't quite what the publisher was looking for. Sometimes, like Selom and his art course, I didn't get there the first time but I did get there later.

Sometimes, the first draft of a story, which I thought was fantastic, was actually a bit confusing, too slow or in need of more research. I had to know that, so I could fix it and make it a really good book rather than just an average one. If I had let failure crush me, I would never have got better and eventually succeeded.

The people in this book have the kinds of job that lots of us want – so there is always competition. But this doesn't mean it can't be YOU who gets that job. Why *not* you? Look at the different routes these people took to get into their careers. It wasn't all plain sailing. Some went to university; some didn't. Most got knockbacks but found a way to try again.

So what next? If you know what you want to do, find the checklist for the job you want and start working on it today. A few years from now, it could really pay off.

And don't worry if you actually haven't got a *clue* what you want to do. Lots of people don't know even as adults. You can have fun finding out what interests you and trying diffcrent things. Or is there anything you love doing *already* that you could do for a job?

Above all, take a deep breath when you fail (and you WILL), work out what you can learn from it and KEEP GOING. Tell yourself that, next time, you'll fail better … and then fail better again … until it's no longer a fail.

Good luck!

Glossary

Achilles tendon: the part of the body that connects the calf muscle to the heel bone

admin: day-to-day organization and management

agents: people who complete tasks for other people

arrange: to adapt music for a special purpose

BBC (British Broadcasting Corporation): an organization that shows radio and TV programmes in Great Britain

broadcast journalist: a person who reports or presents a radio or TV show

caricatures: funny, exaggerated drawings

cash flow: the money coming in and out of a business

choreography: the arrangement of movements for a dance

collection: in fashion, this means a group of clothes designed at the same time for one brand, for example, a spring collection

disillusioned: to be disappointed in something or someone that isn't as good as you had thought they or it would be

feature: a special newspaper article or programme that deals with a particular subject

green room: a room where performers can relax when they are not on set or on stage

Harrods: a large, famous and expensive shop in London

hazmat suit: clothing covering the entire body worn to protect against dangerous substances

instrumentation: the arrangement of instruments used in a piece of music

internship: when someone works (paid or unpaid) to get work experience

invoices: lists of goods sent or work done, with the prices being charged

label: a brand name

literary festivals: events involving talks about books

logistics: the organization of a complicated activity

mic: a microphone

microphone shield: a filter on microphones to help reduce unwanted clicks and crackles

mindset: a way of thinking

open call: an audition open to anyone

PA system (public address system): the equipment for projecting sound

producers: people who organize and supervise TV or radio shows, films or plays

production company: an organization which makes films, TV, plays or radio programmes

publishers: companies that prepare printed or digital materials for sale

resilient: to be able to recover quickly and easily from challenging events

root notes: the first notes of each chord, often the lowest-sounding notes

royalties: the percentage writers get paid from book sales

runner: a person who takes messages and does other small tasks

set: the place where furniture and scenery is, where actors will perform or be filmed

scripts: the texts of plays, films, TV or radio programmes or speeches

session work: when a musician or singer is hired to play or sing in recording sessions

showjumper: a horse trained to jump over obstacles

spread: in publishing, this means a pair of pages (left and right) when the book is opened – in this book, pages 46 and 47 are an example of a spread

storyboards: sets of pictures that show how scenes will be filmed

tap-dancer: a person who taps out a rhythm with their shoes as they dance

textiles: work involved in making fabric

welder: a person who melts materials to join them together

womenswear: clothes for women

Index

actor 6, 29, 34, 36, 47
Allen, Charlotte 24–28
author 5, 8
Bennett, Andy 6, 39–43
celebrity 24, 42
Chader, Hiba 29–33, 44
checklist 8, 13, 18, 23, 28, 33, 38, 43, 45
creative 4, 24, 36
dancer 14–15, 19–21, 23
director 32–36
fail 16, 18, 44–45
fashion designer 24
illustrator 9, 13
McRae, Steven 19–23
perform 18, 22, 36, 47
radio presenter 39, 41
Rycroft, Rebecca 34–38
Sanderson, Hayley 14–18
singer 6, 14–15, 18, 47
Sparkes, Ali 5–8
Sunu, Selom 9–13, 44

48